POCKET PRAYERS
for WOMEN

Simple Prayers
of
Hope

pil Publications International, Ltd.

Natalie Walker Whitlock is the author of more than 500 articles and 13 books, including *Golden Wisdom: Timeless Inspirations* and *A Parent's Guide to the Internet*. She lives with her husband and seven children in Arizona.

Alisa Hope Wagner loves to write across genres about what the Holy Spirit is teaching her. She married her high school sweetheart, and they have three amazing children. You can read her current writings at www.faithimagined.com.

Additional contributors: Nancy Parker Brummett, Elaine Creasman, Christine A. Dallman, June Eaton, Margaret Anne Huffman, Marie D. Jones

Louis Weber, CEO
Publications International, Ltd.
7373 North Cicero Avenue
Lincolnwood, Illinois 60712

Permission is never granted for commercial purposes.

ISBN-13: 978-1-4508-3264-9
ISBN-10: 1-4508-3264-4

Manufactured in China.

8 7 6 5 4 3 2 1

Pray Anywhere, Anytime

Humans have a deep desire to converse with their Creator. Whether we're praising or questioning, we want to reach out to our God.

Pocket Prayers for Women: Simple Prayers of Hope is a tool for daily conversation with God. It includes prayers—both classic and modern—about hope. You will also find brief passages of Scripture and inspirational quotes to help keep you hopeful during good and trying times.

Best of all, this book is small enough to fit in a purse, briefcase, glove box, or nightstand—making it easy for you to take advantage of the awesome privilege of talking with God every day!

A Fresh Start

*For God did not give us a spirit of
cowardice, but rather a spirit of power
and of love and of self-discipline.*
2 Timothy 1:7

*L*ord, I'm looking forward to this
new phase of my life. It is full of
promise and hope, though I know that
challenges will surely come as well. I
know you have all the courage, strength,
faithfulness, and love I need to meet each
moment from a perspective of peace.
I just need to stay tethered to you in
prayer, listening for your Spirit to guide
me and turn my thoughts continually
back toward you. That's the key to a
good life.

Truly New

I am about to do a new thing; now it springs forth, do you not perceive it?

Isaiah 43:19

Lord, the best thing about turning over a new leaf is the word *new*! All the good intentions I have are meaningless unless I am truly new from the inside out. Give me a new attitude, Lord! I need a new focus, a new passion, a new mission—all based on the things you want to do through me.

Strength Beyond My Own

Even youths will faint and be weary,
and the young will fall exhausted;
but those who wait for the Lord
shall renew their strength,
they shall mount up with wings like eagles,
they shall run and not be weary,
they shall walk and not faint.

Isaiah 40:30–31

On days when I find myself feeling old, I like to remember this verse, Lord. I may not have all the physical stamina and endurance I once had, but spiritually you have taught me what it means to tap into a strength far beyond my own—yours.

I witness this otherworldly strength in the way you carry me through trials that at first seemed unbearable. I see it in the day-to-day "small things," such as prayer, that you've helped me to establish in my life. Wings of eagles, indeed! I'm soaring on your strength at this very moment.

Mine, O thou lord of life,
send my roots rain.
—Gerard Manley Hopkins

Second Chances

Our steps are made firm by the Lord,
when he delights in our way;
though we stumble,
we shall not fall headlong,
for the Lord holds us by the hand.

Psalm 37:23–24

tumbling happens. Don't I know it! I can get bummed out just by reviewing my mistakes and mess-ups from the past week. But thankfully, I don't need to! God has hold of my hand. My worst blunders are not the end of the world. God will bring a new day, a fresh start, a redeemed relationship, and a restored soul.

Pray Away!

The Lord is near to all who call on him,
to all who call on him in truth.

Psalm 145:18

Some people feel guilty for resorting to prayers of desperation. But God never turns away anyone who sincerely turns to him for help. Even when we've been distant, not walking close to him, he doesn't despise our cries for help.

So this sheep was lost, so this sheep was
dead, So this soul was dead and from his
own death he is risen from the dead. He
caused the very heart of God to tremble
With the shudder of worry
and with the shudder of hope.

—Charles Péguy

An Illuminated Path

Indeed, you are my lamp, O Lord,
the Lord lightens my darkness.

2 Samuel 22:29

When I leave you behind and try to go about my day without your guidance, Lord, it's like groping around in the dark. I stub my heart on relationship issues. I trip over my ego. I fall down the steps of my foolish choices. How much better to seek the light of your presence first thing and enjoy the benefit of having you illuminate each step of my day!

It is good to embrace a hope.
—Ovid

By God's Grace

My grace is sufficient for you, for power is made perfect in weakness.

2 Corinthians 12:9

Lord, once again I am aware that you, by your grace, gave me the strength to work through a situation that I was woefully unprepared to face. I accept that when we are completely out of ideas, drained of all energy, and so sick at heart we can barely breathe, your grace and strength lift us up and carry us forward. Thank you, Lord.

He Is Risen!

But [the angel] said to [the women],
"Do not be alarmed; you are looking for
Jesus of Nazareth, who was crucified.
He has been raised; he is not here.
Look, there is the place they laid him."

Mark 16:6

Jesus had promised his followers that he would die, and then rise again. Sometimes he spoke in parables, though, and perhaps they thought (or hoped) he was speaking metaphorically. But then on that mind-blowing morning—when Jesus exited his tomb in triumph over our nemesis death—there was no doubt that he had meant what he had said.

"Look!" the angel exclaimed. In other words, "See for yourself that it's true." Jesus has risen, and he opened the way to eternal life for all who trust in him.

But the pains that he endured, Alleluia!
Our salvation have procured, Alleluia!
Now above the sky he's king, Alleluia!
Where the angels ever sing. Alleluia!
—Charles Wesley

Open Our Eyes

Here is the lamb of God
who takes away the sin of the world!

John 1:29

*L*ord, the world just wasn't ready for your appearance by the Jordan. There you were, the King they so desired—yet most didn't know you. Let us welcome you into our world today as wholeheartedly as John the Baptist did! For you came to be our hope and our salvation.

Focus on
the Good and True

Set your minds on things that are above,
not on things that are on earth.

Colossians 3:2

Lord, how easily we are drawn into
the headlines on tabloids while
we stand in line at the grocery store.
How tempting it is to stop to hear the
latest gossip, listening when we shouldn't
and repeating things we don't even
know are true. Distract us from such
things, Lord. Help us to avoid getting too
immersed in the things of this world,
for we know that we are just passing
through on our way to our true home
with you.

Hope for Others

*All praise to God, the Father of our Lord
Jesus Christ. God is our merciful Father
and the source of all comfort. He comforts
us in all our troubles so that we can
comfort others. When they are troubled,
we will be able to give them
the same comfort God has given us.*
2 Corinthians 1:3–4 NLT

*L*ord, only you can take all the
heartaches and failures in our
lives and turn them into compassionate
messages of hope for others. We care
for an aging parent, and so are able
to relate to the needs of the elderly
around us. We go through a divorce,
and we can then give genuine advice

during our interactions with single
mothers. Our pain becomes others'
gain, Lord. Sometimes looking back over
our shoulders brings us hope for the
opportunities that are surely ahead of us.
Thank you for second chances.

*Comfort isn't ours alone—it is to be
shared with those we encounter each day.*

A Comforting Presence

I lift up my eyes to the hills—from where will my help come? My help comes from the Lord, who made heaven and earth.

Psalm 121:1–2

*L*ord, today I pray for all those who are in desperate need of help: victims of earthquakes and tornadoes, the homeless, and the physically and emotionally destitute people of our world. Make yourself known to them, Lord. May they feel the comfort of your presence. You will not leave them without help, nor without hope.

The Joy of the Lord

*With joy you will draw water
from the wells of salvation.*

Isaiah 12:3

When grief fills my heart, Father,
whether I'm feeling loss, shame,
betrayal, or some other sorrow, I know
it's temporary, even though at times it
feels as though it will never go away.
I know that your future for me is joy.
Strengthen me with your joy today,
Father. I need it to lift up my soul.

*Joy is much deeper than mere happiness.
Happiness is like a brook that can dry up
when the sun gets too hot. But joy is like a
vast water system that flows directly from
the Lord—an unfailing source.*

Live the Truth

He changes times and seasons… he gives
wisdom to the wise and knowledge to those
who have understanding.

Daniel 2:21

Lord, sometimes I feel you've blessed me with all kinds of knowledge that no one is interested in hearing! Help me know when and how to share your wisdom with others. Help me to show others your truth, rather than just talk about it. You taught us by living out the truth, Lord. Help us to do the same.

The shortest answer is doing.

—English Proverb

Trust in God

And those who know your name put their
trust in you, for you, O Lord, have not
forsaken those who seek you.

Psalm 9:10

Lord, maybe it's in the times we aren't sure that you are hearing our prayers that we learn to trust you the most. Eventually—in your time—we hear your answer. We know that all our hopes and dreams are safe in your hands. Even when the answer to a prayer is "no," we are comforted by the knowledge that you care about us and respond to our concerns in a way that will ultimately be for our good.

Always by My Side

For this is what the high and lofty One says—he who lives forever, whose name is holy: "I live in a high and holy place, but also with him who is contrite and lowly in spirit, to revive the spirit of the lowly and to revive the heart of the contrite."

Isaiah 57:15 NIV

Lord, in my darkest moments, it is easy to despair and fear that you have given up on me. It would be understandable for you to be angry and leave me to my ruin. How comforting it is to know that the minute I regret what I have done and turn to you, you are right where you have been all along—by my side, ready to embrace and carry me until I am strong enough to take a step on my own. Thank you for your faithfulness, Lord—especially when I least deserve it.

After our examination of conscience, we do often find ourselves unlovable, but it is precisely that which makes us want God—because he is the only one who loves the unlovable.
—Archbishop Fulton Sheen

A New Hope

Just as Christ was raised from the dead by the glory of the Father, so we too might walk in newness of life.

Romans 6:4

Lord, today my heart goes out to all those whose past mistakes weigh them down and make any vision they have of their future dreary at best. Oh, that they might know you and the saving grace you bring! Draw near to them today, Lord. Reveal yourself to them in a way that will reach them, and through your mercy and forgiveness, bestow upon them a new vision—and a new hope.

An Uncluttered Mind

How weighty to me are your thoughts,
O God! How vast is the sum of them!

Psalm 139:17

*L*ord, I want my thoughts to be like
your thoughts. I want to discern
what you discern and have the insight
you have into all that happens in the
world. I know that can never really be,
Lord, but if I am open to your Spirit at
all times, perhaps I can construe your
hopes now and then. May my mind never
be so cluttered that I fail to receive a
message you are trying to share with me.

The knowledge God shares with us
is the deepest knowledge of all.

Nothing to Fear

Even though I walk through the darkest valley, I fear no evil; for you are with me.

Within the valleys of mountainous terrain, darkness lingers long in the morning and swoops down to settle swiftly in the evening. The taller the surrounding mountaintops, the deeper and darker the valley. The psalm writer has one of these deep valleys in mind—a place where the path is shadowy and a chill is always in the air.

Yet here, in what some might call a godforsaken place, the psalm writer surprises us with these words: "I fear no evil; for you are with me." He comforts us with his reminder that when we follow the Lord our shepherd, there is no such thing as a godforsaken place.

If I could choose anyone to be with me in my suffering, in my loneliness, in my sorrow, wouldn't the best choice be the one who discerns all and cares most about me?

Sure and Steady

So let us not grow weary
in doing what is right, for we will reap
at harvest time, if we do not give up.

Galatians 6:9

I appreciate this reminder to keep chugging along the "high road." It can feel like I'm going backward when I see others taking not-so-ethical shortcuts and "getting ahead." These shortcuts are mighty tempting, but a bit of ill-gained ease is not worth forfeiting the fruits of good labor—labor I hope will always honor you, Lord.

It is never too late
to be what you might have been.
—George Eliot

Choose Peace

*Peace I leave with you; my peace I give
to you. I do not give to you as the world
gives. Do not let your hearts be troubled,
and do not let them be afraid.*

John 14:27

This verse leaves the question of my
peace up to me. Will I let my heart
be troubled today? Jesus gave those who
follow him an assurance of his abiding
presence. Will I choose to always give his
peace its place in my soul?

*Take a dip in God's ocean of peace right
now. Lay back, and let the waters of his
love carry you along, as you trust him with
all that may be troubling you.*

Clothed in Salvation

I will greatly rejoice in the Lord,
my whole being shall exult in my God;
for he has clothed me with the garments of
salvation, he has covered me with the robe
of righteousness, . . . as a bride adorns
herself with her jewels.

Isaiah 61:10

What fantastic word pictures! Salvation worn like a garment, and belonging to you revealed as a bride's glittering accessories—that's how you describe my life in you. And yet, sometimes it is hard to see it that way. Give me hope to believe this reality.

Trust God's perspective.

Lasting Peace

Now may the Lord of peace himself
give you peace at all times in all ways.

2 Thessalonians 3:16

Lord, you who brought peace in the midst of the storm are the only one who can bring peace to our world today. The conflicts are not limited to wars on foreign soil--they rage in the hearts and minds of many of us. Be the source of peace in every gathering storm, Lord. You are the Prince of Peace, and we need you desperately.

As on the Sea of Galilee
the Christ is whispering, "Peace."
—John Greenleaf Whittier

Eternal Comfort

Now may our Lord Jesus Christ himself and God our Father, who loved us and through grace gave us eternal comfort and good hope, comfort your hearts and strengthen them in every good work and word.

2 Thessalonians 2:16–17

Sometimes the circumstances of our lives are so difficult, Lord! Often misfortunes seem to come all at once. Other times ongoing, wear-me-down situations or relationships seem to follow us day in and day out. Then there are the crushing tragedies that strike us in our tracks and devastate us. These things do not define a life of faith—but a life of faith is not exempt from them, either.

Suffering is as real for the faithful as for anyone else. However, we have an "eternal comfort and good hope" that lifts us up. In that comfort and hope, God carries us, heals us with the balm of his tender mercies, and strengthens us to carry on in what is good.

Regardless of circumstances today, may you keep the faith within the hope and comfort of Christ's eternal love for you.

Showers of Hope

Let us hold fast to the confession of our hope without wavering, for he who has promised is faithful.

Hebrews 10:23

Lord, I know you are supremely faithful! Today I ask you to restore hope to the hopeless. Plant seeds of hope in hearts that have lain fallow for so long. Send down showers of hope on those struggling with illness, persecution, or difficult relationships. Your hope has the power to sustain us—even when nothing seems the least bit hopeful.

Knowing the source of all hope, may we never be found hopeless.

A Noble Judge

Great and amazing are your deeds,
Lord God the Almighty! Just and true
are your ways, King of the nations!

Revelation 15:3

ord, you are the King of Kings,
and you do all things with perfect
justice. You will not allow evil to prevail.
All people—powerful and peasant, rich
and poor—will be called to give you an
account of how they've lived. Help me to
live well today, honoring you in all I do.

In the eyes of God, the infinite spirit,
all the millions that have lived
and now live do not make a crowd.
He only sees each individual.
—Søren Kierkegaard

An Honest Spirit

*If the anger of the ruler rises against you,
do not leave your post,
for calmness will undo great offenses.*

Ecclesiastes 10:4

*M*ost of us know all too well what that moment is like—the panic that sets in when we realize we've made a major mistake. When we fall out of good graces with the person in charge, life can be very stressful. Such times tempt us to scramble to make amends or to just give up, defeated.

The passage above is a great tip from the top. It was written by the most powerful king ever to rule in Israel.

King Solomon was the person in charge, and here he offers some insight about dealing with such an experience. The king's advice? Don't panic. Be calm. Listen well. Speak with a matter-of-fact, honest spirit. Solomon tells us that such a response will go a long way toward making amends.

Bravery is being the only person who knows you're afraid.
—Franklin P. Jones

Never Far Apart

The Lord watch between you and me,
when we are absent one from the other.

Genesis 31:49

*L*ord, how hard it is to say good-bye to loved ones visiting from far away. Help us be mindful that even on days when we can't see their smiles or feel their hugs, you are lovingly watching over all of us. We are connected in a special way through you, Lord. Spiritually, we are never far apart.

If you pray for me and I pray for you,
God closes the distance between us two.

Future Perfection

I am confident of this, that the one who
began a good work among you will bring it
to completion by the day of Jesus Christ.

Philippians 1:6

Lord, what a comfort it is to know that
you are working to perfect us even on
days when we feel anything but perfect.
One day all creation will be perfected.
How we look forward to that day when
our faith is fully realized, and we are
complete in you!

Be patient with me.
God isn't finished with me yet.

—Anonymous

Come to Me

Draw near to God,
and he will draw near to you.

James 4:8

once heard someone say, "If God seems far away, guess who moved?" It's true, Lord: Sometimes I drift far from you. I neglect reading your Word, I let my prayer life go by the wayside, and I get tangled up in my attempts to handle everything on my own. I usually come to a sudden realization of how much I need you, and I am grateful for the epiphany!

When we take even the littlest step toward God, he closes the gap between us with one giant step toward us.

Overwhelming Needs

I pray that the sharing of your faith may become effective when you perceive all the good that we may do for Christ.

Philemon 1:6

*L*ord, I am often overwhelmed by all the suffering in this world. Through prayer I regain my senses—I know it's not up to me to meet all the needs in the world. Please help me figure out which assignments belong to me; help me to focus on those and entrust the others to you.

We are not called upon to do all the good that is possible, but only that which we can do.

—Mother Theodore Guerin

The Source of My Rescue

*Though the fig tree does not blossom,
and no fruit is on the vines; though the
produce of the olive fails and the fields
yield no food; though the flock is cut off
from the fold and there is no herd in the
stalls, yet I will rejoice in the Lord;
I will exult in the God of my salvation.*

Habakkuk 3:17–18

A modern-day equivalent of this verse might go something like this: Even though the world seems to be in turmoil and I am concerned for the future, I will continue to praise God each day because I know he is the source of my rescue.

God protects me, provides for me, and knows what I need at every moment. Even on the darkest days he is nearby, loving me and sending me strength.

Still round the corner there may wait,
A new road or a secret gate.
—J.R.R. Tolkien

True Comfort

*Then the Lord God will wipe away
the tears from all faces.*

Isaiah 25:8

*L*ord, it hurts to see those we love
with tears in their eyes. We want
so desperately to take away their pain
and comfort them. But as we go to their
sides in their time of need, we should
not go alone. Only you can offer true
comfort. Please add your comfort to ours
as we support our friends through these
trying times.

*God collects the tears we cry,
and each one touches his heart.*

Answers Unveiled

Now I know only in part; then I will know fully, even as I have been fully known.
1 Corinthians 13:12

*L*ord, how long the list of questions I want to ask you in heaven is getting to be! We can't understand so many of the things that happen because we aren't able to see them as you do. Help us remember that the answers will come to light on your schedule.

Our real blessings often appear to us in the shape of pains, losses and disappointments; but let us have patience, and we soon shall see them in their proper figures.
—Joseph Addison

45

Overcoming Anger

You must understand this, my beloved:
let everyone be quick to listen,
slow to speak, slow to anger;
for your anger does not produce
God's righteousness.

James 1:19–20

*L*ord, I have had to experience this truth many times over. How many times has my anger produced regret, Father? More times than I can count. Thomas Jefferson advised counting to ten when angry and to a hundred when very angry. Too often, though, I'm more prone to Mark Twain's approach: "When angry, count four; when very angry, swear."

But I know that's not okay. I want to take the high road as often as possible. I want to be patient when frustrated, dignified when wronged. I confess my slowness to listen, my quickness to speak, and my habit of letting anger rule the moment. Here is a fresh start right now as I receive your forgiveness. Please lead me forward as one who is focused on following in your footsteps.

Trusting Hearts

*And [Abram] believed the Lord; and the
Lord reckoned it to him as righteousness.*

Genesis 15:6

Today I'll simply trust you, Father.
I'll remember that you're not
looking for résumés full of impressive
credentials; rather, you seek hearts that
trust in you. You want to enjoy a vibrant,
meaningful relationship with me—a
relationship in which I trust you fully.
That's the starting point of a life lived
for you.

*Love, trust, and respect are foundational
in any strong relationship,
including my relationship with God.*

Focus on Truth

I do not consider that I have made it my own; but this one thing I do: forgetting what lies behind and straining forward to what lies ahead, I press on towards the goal for the prize of the heavenly call of God in Christ Jesus.

Philippians 3:13–14

*L*ord, what good does it do to dwell on past mistakes? You tell us to look forward, and yet we replay failures in our minds. We know those thoughts aren't from you, Lord.

We don't put photos of our failures in our scrapbooks— why store them in our minds?

Break the Chains

In all these things we are more than
conquerors through him who loved us.

Romans 8:37

*L*ord, today I pray for all those who
suffer from any sort of addiction.
Whether it's gambling, overeating, or
compulsive exercising, addiction keeps
them from being the people you designed
them to be. Their obsession walls them
off from their loved ones. Release them
from their chains, Lord. Give them the
strength to find new life in you.

Consider all the past as nothing, and say,
like David: Now I begin to love my God.
—Francis de Sales

Empowering Strength

Do not be grieved, for the joy of the Lord is your strength.

Nehemiah 8:10

*L*ord, my heart aches for my friend, who is undergoing chemotherapy. How it saps her energy. Sometimes it seems the cure is more devastating than the disease. Stay close to her in this time of healing, Lord. Bring her comfort, and fill her with the knowledge that she can find hope in you. I know you will lend her the strength she needs to get through this trying time.

Nothing heals like the empowering strength that comes through the Lord.

Anything Is Possible

Jesus looked at them and said,
"For mortals it is impossible,
but not for God;
for God all things are possible."

Mark 10:27

*L*ord, how hard it is for us to live in peace with one another. We all have our own ideas about how the world should be, and some topics can be polarizing.

Help us to act in loving ways and to work hard to see and respect others' points of view. We all love this world and you—please help us keep this in mind and work from there.

It is easy to get ahead of ourselves and lose hope; we also know, though, that you are always present, and we truly believe that anything is possible with you.

We place the troubles of our world at your feet. We know you will mold them into something breathtaking.

Will you end wars by asking men to trust men who evidently cannot be trusted? No. Teach them to love and trust God; then they will be able to love the men they cannot trust, and will dare to make peace with them, not trusting in them but in God.

—Thomas Merton

Light the Way

*You show me the path of life. In your
presence there is fullness of joy; in your
right hand are pleasures forevermore.*

Psalm 16:11

Those who don't know you are
missing so much, Lord! Joy is in
your hand, and you are eager to give it
to those who come to you. I pray today
for those who are searching. Please shine
your grace to light their way.

*I've heard it said that telling others
about the Lord doesn't need to be
complicated. Really, it's much like
one pauper showing another pauper
where she has found treasure.*

A Messenger of Hope

To them God chose to make known how great among the Gentiles are the riches of the glory of this mystery, which is Christ in you, the hope of glory.

Colossians 1:27

*L*ord, how it breaks my heart to see pain and loneliness in someone's eyes. Because of the unfolding of your miraculous plan to send your Son to die for us, hopelessness should never take up residence in us! We can be filled with your Spirit so quickly if we just focus on you. Help me bring your hope to those in despair, Lord.

Inscrutable Ways

For everything there is a season,
and a time for every matter under heaven:
a time to be born, and a time to die.

Ecclesiastes 3:1–2

There are few things in life more heartbreaking than the death of a child. One so recently born, exiting life far too soon for our hearts to handle it. There is a time to be born, and a time to die. But there's supposed to be lots of time in between—a lifetime, in fact. How do we pick up the pieces and go on when our hearts ache as they never have before?

O Lord, it is so hard to see the hope in certain circumstances. I guess we just need time. Time to grieve. Time to regain our balance. Time to renew our trust and hope for the future. While we are going through this season of healing, please hold us close.

And the mother gave,
in tears and pain,
The flowers she most did love;
She knew she should find them all again
In the fields of light above.
—Henry Wadsworth Longfellow

Fresh Air

*I acknowledged my sin to you, and I did
not hide my iniquity; I said, "I will confess
my transgressions to the Lord,"
and you forgave the guilt of my sin.*

Psalm 32:5

Confessing our sin to God is like
bursting out into the fresh air
after being stuck a long time in a stifling
room. It frees our soul from the misery
of guilt. Best of all, "coming clean" leads
us back to God, who quickly and lovingly
grants us the forgiveness we long for.

*The only sin God cannot
forgive is the one I neglect
to bring before him.*

Filled with the Spirit

And the life I now live in the flesh
I live by faith in the Son of God,
who loved me and gave himself for me.

Galatians 2:20

Lord, how hopelessly aware we are of our earthly bodies. As we age, they develop frailties—not to mention weird bumps and lumps! But thanks to you, we are so much more than our bodies. For although we live in the flesh, we are filled with your Spirit. Thank you for that perspective, Lord. It makes it so much easier to watch our earthly bodies begin to fail. How ready we will be to exchange them for the heavenly models!

Reshape Me

We are the clay, and you are our potter;
we are all the work of your hand.

Isaiah 64:8

ere we are again, Lord. Another time when I feel like I've made a complete and utter mess of this life you've given me. I place myself in your hands. If you need to totally reshape me to turn me into someone more useful, so be it! Thank you for not abandoning me, your humble creation. Make me over in your design.

Only God can give us a perfect makeover
from the inside out.

An Open Mind

*O Lord, you will hear the desire of the
meek; you will strengthen their heart,
you will incline your ear to do justice
for the orphan and the oppressed.*

Psalm 10:17–18

*L*ord, please slow me down and
open my senses to the needs of
those around me. Too often I breeze by
people with an offhand greeting but
remain in a cocoon of my own concerns.
Help me find ways to be of service.

*If we were supposed to talk
more than we listen, we would have
two mouths and one ear.*

—Mark Twain

Inner Freedom

*Jesus said to the people
who believed in him, "You are truly my
disciples if you remain faithful to my
teachings. And you will know the truth,
and the truth will set you free."*
John 8:31–32 NLT

What kind of freedom do you mean, Lord? There are people in jail cells in some countries because they have chosen to live according to your Word. Some of your other faithful followers struggle with illness or disability.

When you speak of freedom, you must mean something beyond a free body. I think you mean the spiritual freedom we enjoy in you. This freedom loosens any worldly bonds and holds the promise of eternal life in heaven. There the last vestiges of restraint will disappear, and our freedom will be complete.

The inner freedom we enjoy now in Christ is just a taste of what we will enjoy for all eternity.

The Essence of Self

Creator, help me to remember who I am. Before I became a friend, there was me. Before I started my career, there was me. Before I found the love of my life, there was me. Guide me back to my specific essence. Restore my wholeness, so that I can become a better friend, a better colleague—a better woman.

Coming into wholeness as a woman isn't so much about discovering who you are, but about taking back the parts of yourself you gave away.

—Barbara D'Angelis

Genuine Peace

Blessed are the peacemakers,
for they will be called children of God.

Matthew 5:9

Father, you are the greatest
peacemaker. You made
reconciliation with humanity possible by
means of great personal sacrifice—but
without compromising the truth. Help
me follow your example. Grant me the
courage and wisdom to work toward real
peace, which values all people and fulfills
our need for truth and love.

Peace prevails when individuals
value the needs and ideas of others
as much as their own.

The Right Direction

*There is therefore now no condemnation
for those who are in Christ Jesus.
For the law of the Spirit of life
in Christ Jesus has set you free
from the law of sin and of death.*

Romans 8:1–2

A wise friend once gave me some
advice I have come back to again
and again over the course of my life. I
was having trouble getting past some
mistakes I had made, and my friend
advised me to ask myself, "Am I feeling
condemned by the devil, or am I being
convicted by God's Spirit?"

Condemnation, she told me, is never from
God. "The devil will try to make you feel

like you're just plain worthless," she said. "The Holy Spirit, by contrast, will direct you to confess your wrongdoing, receive God's forgiveness, make amends where you can, and get going in the right direction."

God never condemns his children. His gracious method is to get us back on track as quickly as possible.

Teach Us Contentment

Ye have wept in the ears of the Lord.

Numbers 11:18 KJV

A phrase uttered often in our world is "It's not fair!" Are things really often unfair, or do we expect things to be too easy? Just as the Israelites complained while being fed in the wilderness, we sometimes complain when gratification is delayed for mere moments.

Lord of peace, wrap us in your love, and dispel the cloud of discontent that looms over us. Guard us from weeping in your ear. Cleanse our complaining spirits by sprinkling us with your gentle rain of forgiveness.

Courage and Hope

Be strong, and let your heart take courage,
all you who wait for the Lord.

Psalm 31:24

*L*ord, let me be strong today,
drawing my courage from my
hope in you. Help me lean not on my
own strength but on your limitless
power. I know there is work to be done—
burdens to be lifted, temptations to be
resisted, unkindness to be forgiven. Let
my thoughts and actions be motivated by
the hope generated by your promises.

Like the lighthouse beacon,
faith guides our way through the fog
of fear, doubt, and uncertainty
to the seas of clarity beyond.

Hope Exposed

"Did I ask you for a son, my lord?"
she said. "Didn't I tell you,
'Don't raise my hopes'?"

2 Kings 4:28 NIV

*T*he prophet Elisha wants to do something special for a woman who has continuously blessed his ministry. When he asks what she would like, she tells him that there is nothing she needs. Elisha does a little research and finds that she never had a son; he then tells the woman that she will give birth to a son in one year's time.

Instead of rejoicing, the woman cries in fear. Her hope for a son died long ago, and she's terrified to expose herself to more heartbreak.

The weight of hope can be heavy on our souls, and many times we will want to give up on our dreams. But until our yearnings change or subside, we must keep our hope in God's timing and plans. It is okay to raise our hopes in a God who can perform miracles.

Lord, even when I seem to have nothing left, I know I still have hope in you. I trust that you understand me and know the deepest desires of my heart.

Keep Going

Rejoice in hope, be patient in suffering,
persevere in prayer.

Romans 12:12

*L*ord, some days I juggle my
responsibilities flawlessly, but then
one of those days comes along. I arrive
at work late, only to realize we have an
important meeting, and I am woefully
unprepared. I finally get home after
working late, and I am met with the
news that a loved one is in trouble. I feel
like a failure on days like this, Lord. Fill
me with the hope that only you can give.

It's always too early to quit.
—Norman Vincent Peale

Plow in Hope

Surely he says this for us, doesn't he?
Yes, this was written for us, because whoever
plows and threshes should be able to do so
in the hope of sharing in the harvest.

1 Corinthians 9:10 NIV

Have you ever seen a farmer plow, plant, and then try to harvest the very next day? That would be a pretty silly farmer! Yet sometimes we think we can get a "harvest" without the time and effort it takes to plow, plant, and wait patiently for a ripe harvest.

Lord, today I will plant a few seeds,
nurture ones I have already planted,
and "plow in hope"
while I wait for harvest day.

Purify Me

Blessed are the pure in heart,
for they will see God.

Matthew 5:8

How can I achieve purity of heart, Lord? I certainly don't always have right thoughts and motives.

Perhaps I can achieve purity of heart through being honest. I can make it a point to focus on what is right and true and good, continually turning my heart toward you to find those things and be renewed in them.

Please purify my heart
as I stay close to you today, Lord.

Peace of Mind

Take my yoke upon you, and learn from me;
for I am gentle and humble in heart,
and you will find rest for your souls.

Matthew 11:29

*L*ord, if ever there was a day when I needed your rest, it is today. Nothing seems to be going right, and just carrying around my to-do list is exhausting—it is so long! Please help me sort out which things really need to be done and which I can let go.

A wise woman trades her
to-do list for the Lord's.

Let Go

*Cast all your anxiety on him,
because he cares for you.*

1 Peter 5:7

Fretting produces nothing but
overblown what-if scenarios in
our minds. We end up suffering appetite
loss when we need to be keeping up
our strength and sleeplessness when we
should be resting.

How do we get off this treadmill of
worry? We do just what this verse tells
us to do: We take our big ol' bundle of
fears and frets and hand them over to
God. We say, "This is clearly too much for
me to handle. Please help me with this

situation, Lord." We know that if we do this, it will all work out for the best on God's timetable.

Lord, I might have to remind myself 100 times today to leave my cares with you, but each reminder will help make it a habit. Soon I will need to remind myself only 50 times, and it won't be long until I won't need any reminders—I'll simply know that you're in control, and all will come to fruition on your schedule.

Heavenly Binds

May the God of peace himself sanctify you entirely; and may your spirit and soul and body be kept sound and blameless at the coming of our Lord Jesus Christ. The one who calls you is faithful, and he will do this.
1 Thessalonians 5:23–24

Maybe it's bitterness. Maybe it's pride. Or maybe we tend to complain. Whatever sins we struggle with, we should never lose heart! Often it's our weaknesses that keep us close to God. When we find ourselves overwhelmed, it's a signal that we're not devoting enough time to prayer. God is faithful, and through him we can overcome any weakness.

Open Your Heart

*What woman having ten silver coins, if she
loses one of them, does not light a lamp,
sweep the house, and search carefully...?
When she has found it, she calls together
her friends and neighbors, saying, "Rejoice
with me, for I have found the coin that I
had lost." Just so, I tell you, there is joy in
the presence of the angels of God over one
sinner who repents.*

Luke 15:8–10

These verses fill my heart with hope,
Lord. It is so comforting to think of
you searching tirelessly to find me. Grant
me your grace so I can stay on your
paths more steadily.

Active Faith

Prepare your minds for action;
discipline yourselves; set all your hope
on the grace that Jesus Christ
will bring you when he is revealed.

1 Peter 1:13

Father, your Word makes it clear
that the life of faith is not passive.
While we wait for you to answer prayer,
we must keep our minds sharp and our
hearts strengthened by reading
and studying your Word and by
finding encouragement among
other believers. Our souls need
these disciplines to stay focused
on ever-present hope.

Unchanging Perfection

Jesus Christ is the same yesterday and today and forever.

Hebrews 13:8

*L*ord, what comfort we find in your changeless nature. When we look back and remember all the ways you've guided us in the past, we know we have no need to be anxious about the future. You were, are, and always will be our Savior and Lord. Why should we fear instability when you are always here with us?

Change is a constant part of life, but Jesus is a changeless part of eternity.

Lost Again

But the tax collector, standing far off,
would not even look up to heaven
but was beating his breast and saying,
"God, be merciful to me, a sinner!"

Luke 18:13

*L*ord, on my worst days, I find it comforting to call this parable to mind. On such days I really relate to the tax collector. I feel lost in this world, far from you. Please help me, Lord. Forgive my recent failings and give me the courage, strength, and wisdom to make things right again.

> *Do not lose courage in considering*
> *your own imperfections.*
> —Francis de Sales

Strength in the Lord

For God alone my soul waits in silence;
from him comes my salvation. He alone is
my rock and my salvation, my fortress;
I shall never be shaken.

Psalm 62:1–2

Lord, I pray for those who have sought the wrong kinds of protection. It's so easy for us to become obsessed with protecting our marriages, our children, and our well-being to the extent that we are in danger of losing our peace of mind. Remind us, Lord, that when we are in your hands, we are in the best of hands. With you, we stand strong and have great hope.

The Lord's Vessel

Therefore be imitators of God,
as beloved children, and live in love, as
Christ loved us and gave himself up for us,
a fragrant offering and sacrifice to God.
Ephesians 5:1–2

*L*ord, from the past weeks I'd like to save in the scrapbook of my life just those days that brought you glory... days when in spite of my self-absorption and often worldly focus, you were able to accomplish something through me. Those are the days I cherish, Lord. Help me to move into the next weeks more available—more open—to living such scrapbook-worthy days.

Divine Timing

But when the fullness of time had come,
God sent his Son, born of a woman, born
under the law, in order to redeem those
who were under the law, so that we might
receive adoption as children.

Galatians 4:4–5

Father, it's as if time itself was aware of your plan to redeem humanity through your son. Nothing you do is by happenstance; Jesus came at precisely the right time in history to carry out your purposes.

Father, I trust you with the timing in my life as well. You see things in the light of eternity, and I know you have an amazing plan.

Spiritual Darkness

The people who walked in darkness
have seen a great light; those who lived
in a land of deep darkness—on them
light has shined.

Isaiah 9:2

Isaiah wrote a number of inspired words that pointed to the coming of Christ. In this passage, he speaks of a great light shining on those living in a dark land. Spiritual darkness is the deepest kind of darkness. One may live in physical darkness yet have the light of Christ, which brings joy and hope. Without the light of Christ, something is missing in the soul.

A Message of Hope

Take heart . . . your sins are forgiven.

Matthew 9:2

*F*ather, this passage reminds us about forgiveness and trying again when we have failed. We are thankful that you are a God of second chances. Just as you love us unconditionally, there is nothing our loved ones could do to make us withhold our love. Help us spread the hopeful message that there is no need for despair; forgiveness and a new start are always possible.

I have felt assured that I do not have to fear the future because God is already there.

—Fran Caffey Sandin, *See You Later, Jeffrey*

A Moment of Quiet

*I can do all things through him
who strengthens me.*

Philippians 4:13

Lord, I am overwhelmed by the whirl of activity around me. Getting ready for work, making meals, doing dishes, cleaning house, running errands, fielding phone calls, keeping appointments, dealing with calamities... how do I fit it all in? I am buckling under the weight of each day, only to find that I must get up and start all over again the next.

Father, you are a God of peace and tranquility. I long to find a time to sit

down and talk to you. Show me a quiet
place in the midst of the frenzy, where
I may commune with you, be refreshed,
and know that through your strength,
I can accomplish all that you have in
store for me to do today.

*I must faithfully, patiently, lovingly
and happily do my part—
then quietly wait for God to do His.*
—Ruth Bell Graham,
Prodigals and Those Who Love Them

Choices

*He will yet fill your mouth with laughter,
and your lips with shouts of joy.*

Job 8:21

There is a choice, O God, when
someone cuts me off in traffic, a
loved one leaves dirty socks in the middle
of the floor, or a child leaves a crayon
mark on a wall. I can scream or chuckle. I
know which choice you prefer. Be with me
as I laugh my way into a better mood.

*Angry people usually take life too seriously,
so relax. Loosen up. Look at
the big picture. Let go of your anger.
In light of eternity, it's not worth spending
your short time on earth being angry.*
—Kent Crockett, *The 911 Handbook*

Take the First Step

Bear with one another and, if anyone has a complaint against another, forgive each other; just as the Lord has forgiven you, so you also must forgive.

Colossians 3:13

I got into a silly quarrel with the love of my life, O God of peacemaking and love, and we are having a hard time making up. Please take each of us by the hand and inspire us toward compromise. Amen.

To love someone is to see a miracle invisible to others.
—François Mauriac

The Barren Tree

At least there is hope for a tree:
If it is cut down, it will sprout again,
and its new shoots will not fail.

Job 14:7 NIV

*L*ord, lately I really do feel like a
tree that has been chopped down.
Everything that I've held dear has been
taken from me; I feel numb, and my life
seems meaningless. Hope seems far away.

I have not forgotten, though, that you
are a God of new life. I trust that the
sun will shine again and the rain will fall
when necessary. It is hard to let go of
what was, but I believe that I will grow
strong and my heart will again leap for

joy rather than merely throb with this dull ache.

My roots are secure in you, Lord—I will not allow myself to remain so shaken. Though the storms of this life uproot and tear down, I will hold steadfast to hope.

*Lord, please grant me the strength
to start each day with hope
until the days truly turn joyful.*

Victorious Praise

Why, my soul, are you downcast?
Why so disturbed within me? Put your
hope in God, for I will yet praise him,
my Savior and my God.

Psalm 42:5 NIV

Many times I feel that I have the right to be downcast. But God's Word says that we should not be downcast because we have an amazing hope through him. If I focus on this hope, joy will enter my spirit, and my negative emotions will disperse.

I will no longer allow myself to have a disturbed soul. I have only one life on this earth, and I choose to live it victoriously.

Wonder-Filled Days

So if anyone is in Christ, there is a new creation; everything old has passed away; see, everything has become new!

2 Corinthians 5:17

Children leap from sleep and skip into a wonder-filled day—assuming it will be one! See how they jump up after a fall or rise after disappointment, knowing more good than bad sums up each day. Ah, an example to follow!

My candle burns at both ends;
It will not last the night;
But ah, my foes, and oh, my friends—
It gives a lovely light!
—Edna St. Vincent Millay, "First Fig"

Plans, Not Alarms

You grew weary from your many
wanderings, but you did not say, "It is
useless." You found your desire rekindled,
and so you did not weaken.

Isaiah 57:10

Galvanize me into prevention,
intervention, and rebuilding your
creation, Lord. This world needs fixers—
not just worriers and those prone to
panic. It needs concrete plans, not just
alarms. Let hope, not fear, always be the
message I relate.

When life's taken its best shot,
dig in and lift eyes skyward. Feel it?
That's God's spirit blowing across
weary lives, filling us with a second wind.

The Help That Is Needed

Don't get tired of helping others. You will be rewarded when the time is right, if you don't give up.

Galatians 6:9 CEV

Over and over I ask myself, "What can I do?" What can I do to make a difference? One of the hardest things about reaching out is having others think I can "fix it" and then finding out that I can't. Lord, help me to remember that what you promise is not to "fix it" for us but rather to give us whatever it takes to prevail in spite of our hurts. Help me keep in mind that sometimes all that is necessary is a listening ear.

Fruits Grown in Hope

*May the God of hope fill you with all joy
and peace as you trust in him,
so that you may overflow with hope
by the power of the Holy Spirit.*

Romans 15:13 NIV

As I trust in you, God, I know you
will fill my life with your hope.
That hope will transcend into every area
of my soul, and beautiful buds of joy and
peace will begin to grow. I want your joy
and peace to be obvious in my life.

I'm tired of pretending to be joyful and
acting like I'm peaceful. I desire those
fruits to grow naturally, out of the
wellspring of hope in my heart.

Prod me to trust you at all times, Lord, and to rely on your Word. I know that my joy and peace are complete in you, and I have hope that you can work in me despite my weaknesses.

I'm done with putting my hope into the changing tides of this world. I'm ready to put all of my hope in you, so real fruits of joy and peace can grow.

A Sure Source of Help

My help comes from the Lord,
who made heaven and earth.

Psalm 121:2

*Y*ou give your help, O Lord, not in proportion to our merit, but based only on your generosity and wise judgment. For you come not only to those who are "keeping it together," but to those of us who are fragmented and fractured. I need to feel your tender presence so that I know I am never alone—even in my weakest moments.

Trust the past to God's mercy,
the present to God's love,
and the future to God's providence.
—Augustine of Hippo

An Anchor to the Soul

We who have taken refuge might be strongly encouraged to seize the hope set before us. We have this hope, as a sure and steadfast anchor of the soul.

Hebrews 6:18–19

Hope is an anchor to the soul. It can keep us from drifting aimlessly, getting caught in whirlpools, or running into sandbars. This anchor is essential in a world so full of various waves. Sometimes those waves slap us from behind; sometimes we see them coming but cannot get out of the way. In all cases, hope ties us to safety. The waves come and go in their fury or playfulness—but hope is always there.

Between Faith and Love

And now faith, hope, and love abide,
these three…

1 Corinthians 13:13

It can be tempting to write hope off as weak. We often hear, "I hope it doesn't rain." Using hope in this way is mere wishing with no power behind it.

And yet, hope matters. Hope, love, and faith are closely related. Paul listed these specific three for a reason. They are the inseparable sister virtues, each one stronger through association with the other two. A faithful woman is all the stronger if she is also a hopeful woman; and the faithful, hopeful woman is all the more complete if she is also a loving woman. When used together, these beautiful qualities multiply their power and result in immense strength.

Faith lifts the staggering soul on one side,
Hope supports it on the other.
Experience says it must be,
and Love says—let it be.
—Elizabeth Ann Seton

Divine Plans

For a child has been born for us,
a son given to us; authority rests upon his
shoulders; and he is named
Wonderful Counselor, Mighty God,
Everlasting Father, Prince of Peace.

Isaiah 9:6

Jesus fulfilled many roles during his earthly life. When friends ran out of wine at a wedding, Mary asked Jesus to do something. Jesus hesitated because he wasn't sure it was time for him to draw such attention to himself. He soon acquiesced, however, realizing that his time had, indeed, come.

May we follow Jesus' example and always
be open to your plans for our lives, Lord.

A Parched Spirit

The Lord is near to all who call on him,
to all who call on him in truth.

Psalm 145:18

Lord, I thank you for your faithfulness. Your promise to be near me and to hear my prayers gives me comfort and hope. I need your continual guidance. No matter how hopeless a situation may seem, I know you have the answers I need. As I pray, I feel your peace filling up my parched spirit and bringing sweet relief. I feel your wisdom directing my thoughts toward new ideas and solutions. Forgive me, Lord, for the times I have prayed selfishly or have failed to pray at all.

Our Refuge and Strength

*God is our refuge and strength,
an ever-present help in trouble.*

Psalm 46:1 NIV

The familiar story of Job reminds us that as sure as the sparks fly upward, human beings are born to trouble. My time of trouble is here, Lord. I thank you for temporary relief—for giving me respite so I could gather strength for the next battle.

But my sorrow is great, Father, and I cannot find a way out of this troubling situation. My heart is heavy as I look into the future and see nothing but darkness. I am afraid both for myself and for my loved ones.

I know, though, that you take our burdens as your own. You are our refuge and strength. I will cling to you in this time of trouble, knowing you can lead me out of the darkness and into the light.

> *God does not offer us*
> *a way out of the testings of life.*
> *He offers us a way through.*
> —W. T. Purkiser

Woman, Giver of Life

Her children arise and call her blessed.

Proverbs 31:28 NIV

I am woman, giver of life.
I am mother, wife, friend,
and family member.
I am neighbor and concerned
citizen.
I am pregnant with possibilities for
the future and remembrances of
the past.
I give birth to children and to new
ideas.
I nurture everyone around me and
empower them to be their best.
I am a lover, an adventurer, a
guardian angel.
I am woman, giver of life.

Perfect Rest

My soul finds rest in God alone.

Psalm 62:1 NIV

*L*ord, I believe a rest remains
To all Thy people known;
A rest where pure enjoyment reigns,
And Thou art loved alone;
A rest where all our soul's desire
Is fixed on things above,
where fear, and sin, and grief expire,
Cast out by perfect love.

—Charles Wesley

A Longing for Comfort

*Blessed be the God and Father of our Lord
Jesus Christ, the Father of mercies and
the God of all consolation, who consoles
us in all our affliction, so that we may
be able to console those who are in any
affliction with the consolation with which
we ourselves are consoled by God.*

2 Corinthians 1:3–4

*L*ike aching bones that find relief in
a steamy, hot bath, O God, that's
the comfort I hope for. I long for you to
take from my life all the fear, the hurt,
the doubt, the unknown, the insecurity—
every affliction.

I realize, though, that your promise is to
comfort us in our afflictions, not remove

them. Help me to remember that I will experience relief in due time.

There are times when all of us feel comfortless and helpless, but there is great strength in remembering the one who abides with us.
—Charles L. Allen, *Victories in the Valleys of Life*

Abounding in Hope

May the God of hope fill you
with all joy and peace in believing,
so that you may abound in hope
by the power of the Holy Spirit.

Romans 15:13

*L*ord, help me remember that you are the God of hope. You don't want me to feel sad or hopeless. It isn't your plan for me to live in fear or doubt. Help me to feel and access the power of the Holy Spirit. I know that through your Spirit I will find the hope and joy and peace you have promised to your people.

We must accept finite disappointment,
but we must never lose infinite hope.

—Dr. Martin Luther King Jr.

Divine Comfort

Hope deferred makes the heart sick,
but a desire fulfilled is a tree of life.

Proverbs 13:12

We all know the sting of being heartsick. Loss, unrequited love, unfulfilled expectations—any of these can lead to the feeling of our heart literally being sick.

The passage above tells us that it is actually deferring, or putting off, hope that truly makes our hearts sick. God knows the pain we experience in this life. He knows how to comfort us. If we cling to hope and turn to God, despite all that life may throw at us, we are sure to find ourselves filled with peace and joy.

Don't Worry

Therefore I tell you, do not worry about your life, what you will eat or what you will drink, or about your body, what you will wear. Is not life more than food, and the body more than clothing?

Matthew 6:25

*L*oving God, I confess that I worry too much. I worry about the welfare of my loved ones. I worry about my job. I worry about my budget, which seems to be buckling a bit more every month. I even worry about worrying!

Forgive my doubts—my lack of faith and trust in you, O Lord. Teach me to express my needs to you daily in prayer and to trust in your power to help me address all my problems.

In my heart I truly know you will never abandon me. With you in charge of our lives, my loved ones will never want for anything. You take care of all your creations—even the smallest birds and the tiniest flowers.

When you worry, you are borrowing problems that may never happen.

True Contentment

*I have learned to be content
with whatever I have.*

Philippians 4:11

Contentment is hard to learn. But I know, Lord, that you can give me peace in every circumstance and the contentment it brings as I submit to your lordship. Teach me to trust you for each day's problems and rely on you to strengthen me for every task. I can be content as long as I know you are with me, helping me at every turn.

—Charles Stanley, *A Touch of His Peace*

Divine Presence

Lord, sometimes I worry about my loved ones. Though I often complain of the monotony of my day-to-day life, I know my days are full of moments to be treasured. When I hear shocking, horrific stories on the news, I often wonder how I would handle such events if they were to befall me or a loved one.

Father, I cling to your promise that you give each of us a future filled with hope. I am grateful that you hear me when I come to you in prayer. Please stay close to me and my loved ones. Grant us the strength to prevail in all circumstances.

An Unfailing Refuge

The wind blows where it chooses,
and you hear the sound of it,
but you do not know where it comes from
or where it goes. So it is with everyone
who is born of the Spirit.

John 3:8

When the winds of change and challenge blow hard into my life, I will take refuge in you, O Lord my God. When the darkness descends upon my home, I will fear not, for I will place my faith in you, Lord.

When a loved one is ill or hurt, I will remain steadfast, for I know that you will be right there among us, Lord.

Although I cannot see you, I know you are always with me, and in that I take great comfort and find immense strength.

There is no great and no small
To the Soul that maketh all;
And where it cometh, all things are;
And it cometh everywhere.
—Ralph Waldo Emerson

A Cheerful, Hopeful Heart

This is the day that the Lord has made;
let us rejoice and be glad in it.

Psalm 118:24

*L*ord, may I be wakeful at sunrise to begin a new day for you, cheerful at sunset for having done my work for you; thankful at moonrise and under starshine for the beauty of the universe. And may I add what little may be in me to your great world.

—The Abbot of Greve

Seeds of Hope

May those who sow in tears
reap with shouts of joy.

Psalm 126:5

Lord, some days it seems that every hour is spent in toil, with little time left over for enjoying time with loved ones. Help us keep in mind that our hours of work sow seeds of hope. In time, you will comfort us with a posture of joy and celebration. Thank you, Lord, for understanding both our need to work hard and our need to enjoy this beautiful life you gave us.

Only God can replace grief with pure joy!

Hope Makes Us Happy

*Happy are those whose help
is the God of Jacob, whose hope
is in the Lord their God.*

Psalm 146:5

The Psalmist knew that with and through hope, we can find happiness in this life. Even though the principle of hope is a spiritual one, extending into eternity, it can also sustain us through the everyday challenges of life. We can, through hope, bring the strength of heaven into our homes, our workplaces, our minds, and our hearts. Our hope in God's promises empowers us with an eternal perspective.

Child, even this day, trust!
And to-morrow have faith,
And on all to-morrows!
The darkness grows less.
Trust! And each day
when first gleams
the dawn-breath,
Awake thou to pray;
God is wakeful to bless!
—Victor Hugo, "Trust in God"

Never Alone

He will dwell with them…
he will wipe every tear from their eyes.

Revelation 21:3–4

*L*ord, on days when everything seems to go wrong, help me to remember that you are always nearby to offer comfort. It is easy to get overwhelmed and feel lost and alone in this world, but deep down I know that is never the case. You are always at the ready to help—I just need to remember to take a moment to stop, breathe, and pray.

Trials strengthen us
and bring us closer to God.

Divine Light

For it is the God who said, "Let light shine out of darkness," who has shone in our hearts to give the light of the knowledge of the glory of God in the face of Jesus Christ.

2 Corinthians 4:6

*L*ord, your Word is so alive—so vibrant—that it almost seems illuminated when I am reading it. When I am troubled, opening the Bible is like turning on a comforting light in a dark, gloomy room. Thank you, Lord, for loving us so much that you gave us your wisdom to illuminate our lives.

The Bible is the perfect instruction manual for life.

Choose Hope

But the Lord will be the hope of his people,
and the strength of the children of Israel.

Joel 3:16 KJV

*L*iving in difficult times requires us to maintain a positive, hopeful attitude about the future. Having hope is vital for our mental, physical, and spiritual health.

Lord, help me move into the future with a steadfast spirit, looking forward in faith and hope and trusting in the promises you have made to your people.

Today I make a covenant to you that I will choose hope. If I encounter disappointment, I will choose hope. If confronted with temptation, I will choose hope. In the face of fear, I will choose hope. If I sense doubt washing over me, I will choose hope. If I feel angry, I will choose hope. Instead of giving in to sadness or despair, I will choose hope.

In all things that come my way today, Lord, I am determined to choose hope. Regardless of what happened in the past, today—through you—I am strong enough to choose hope.

He who trusts himself is lost.
He who trusts in God can do all things.
—Alphonsus Liguori

Acknowledgments:

"First Fig" from *Collected Poems* by Edna St. Vincent Millay, HarperCollins. Copyright © 1922, 1950 by Edna St. Vincent Millay.

Unless otherwise noted, all Scripture quotations are taken from the *New Revised Standard Version* of the Bible. Copyright © 1989 National Council of the Churches of Christ in the United States of America. Used by permission. All rights reserved.

Scripture quotations marked CEV are from the *Contemporary English Version*. Copyright © 1991, 1992, 1995 by American Bible Society. Used by permission.

Scripture quotations marked KJV are taken from *The Holy Bible, King James Version*.

Scripture quotations marked NIV are taken from *The Holy Bible, New International Version*®, NIV®. Copyright © 1973, 1978, 1984 by Biblica, Inc.™ Used by permission of Zondervan. All rights reserved worldwide. www.zondervan.com

Scripture quotations marked NLT are taken from the *Holy Bible, New Living Translation*, copyright © 1996, 2004, 2007 by Tyndale House Foundation. Used by permission of Tyndale House Publishers, Inc., Carol Stream, Illinois 60188. All rights reserved.

Cover Art: Shutterstock.com

Interior Art: Artville, Brand X Pictures, Jupiterimages Unlimited, Photodisc, Shutterstock.com